for Advent and the Christmas Season 2017–18

SACRED SPACE

December 3, 2017 to January 8, 2018

from the website www.sacredspace.ie

Prayer from the Irish Jesuits

LOYOLA PRESS.
A JESUIT MINISTRY
Chicago

LOYOLA PRESS.
A JESUIT MINISTRY

3441 N. Ashland Avenue
Chicago, Illinois 60657
(800) 621-1008
www.loyolapress.com

Scripture quotations are from *New Revised Standard Version Bible: Catholic Edition*, copyright © 1989, 1993 National Council of the Churches of Christ in the United States of America. Used by permission. All rights reserved.

Advent retreat by Stephen Hoyland, used with permission.

Cover art credit: © iStock/Qweek

ISBN: 978-0-8294-4581-7

17 18 19 20 21 Versa 10 9 8 7 6 5 4 3 2 1

Contents

The Presence of God

Bless all who worship you, almighty God,
from the rising of the sun to its setting:
from your goodness enrich us,
by your love inspire us,
by your Spirit guide us,
by your power protect us,
in your mercy receive us,
now and always.

How to Use This Booklet

During each week of Advent, begin by reading the "Something to think and pray about each day this week." Then go through "The Presence of God," "Freedom," and "Consciousness" steps to help you prepare yourself to hear the word of God speaking to you. In the next step, "The Word," turn to the Scripture reading for each day of the week. Inspiration points are provided if you need them. Then return to the "Conversation" and "Conclusion" steps. Follow this process every day of Advent.

The Advent retreat at the back of this book follows a similar structure: an invitation to experience stillness, a Scripture passage and reflection points, and suggestions for prayer; you may find it useful to move back and forth between the daily reflections and the retreat.

The First Week of Advent
December 3—December 9, 2017

Something to think and pray about each day this week:

Part of the Bigger Plan

I've often thought about the angel coming to Mary. Our feasts and songs and icons celebrate the Annunciation, but I'd never thought about the moment when it was all over. I can only imagine it was something like what writer Annie Dillard experienced when she looked out on what she imagined was a field of angels. "I stood in pieces," she writes, "afraid I was unable to move. Something had unhinged the world." Later she describes the grave and stricken silence, the "unbearable green" and the "God-blasted, paralyzed" fields. People always comment on the bravery of Mary's yes. I never quite understood this. Wouldn't anyone say yes to an angel? But it seems unspeakably brave when I picture that later moment, when Mary stood before the God-blasted, paralyzed day and watched the angel depart.

—Amy Andrews, *2017: A Book of Grace-Filled Days*

The Presence of God

"Be still and know that I am God." Lord, your words lead us to the calmness and greatness of your presence.

Freedom

I am free. When I look at these words in writing, they seem to create in me a feeling of awe. Yes, a wonderful feeling of freedom. Thank you, God.

Consciousness

At this moment, Lord, I turn my thoughts to you.
I will leave aside my chores and preoccupations.
I will take rest and refreshment in your presence, Lord.

The Word

The word of God comes down to us through the Scriptures. May the Holy Spirit enlighten my mind and my heart to respond to the gospel teachings. (Please turn to the Scripture on the following pages. Inspiration points are there should you need them. When you are ready, return here to continue.)

Conversation
Begin to talk with Jesus about the Scripture you have just read. What part of it strikes a chord in you? Perhaps the words of a friend—or some story you have heard recently—will slowly rise to the surface of your consciousness. If so, does the story throw light on what the Scripture passage may be trying to say to you?

Conclusion
Glory be to the Father, and to the Son, and to the Holy Spirit,
As it was in the beginning, is now and ever shall be,
World without end. Amen.

Sunday 3rd December
First Sunday of Advent
Mark 13:33–37

Beware, keep alert; for you do not know when the time will come. It is like a man going on a journey, when he leaves home and puts his slaves in charge, each with his work, and commands the doorkeeper to be on the watch. Therefore, keep awake—for you do not know when the master of the house will come, in the evening, or at midnight, or at cockcrow, or at dawn, or else he may find you asleep when he comes suddenly. And what I say to you I say to all: Keep awake.

- Jesus is speaking of his second coming at the end of time. We must live so that it does not matter when he comes. Our life becomes a preparation for the vision of happiness.

- Do I anticipate the Lord's coming, or do I dread it? Why do I feel as I do about this?

Monday 4th December
Matthew 8:5–11

When [Jesus] entered Capernaum, a centurion came to him, appealing to him and saying, "Lord, my servant is lying at home paralyzed, in terrible distress." And he said to him, "I will come and cure him." The centurion answered, "Lord, I am not worthy to have you come under my roof; but only speak the word, and my servant will be healed. For I also am a man under authority, with soldiers under me; and I say to one, 'Go,' and he goes, and to another, 'Come,' and he comes, and to my slave, 'Do this,' and the slave does it." When Jesus heard him, he was amazed and said to those who followed him, "Truly I tell you, in no one in Israel have I found such faith. I tell you, many will come from east and west and will eat with Abraham and Isaac and Jacob in the kingdom of heaven."

• This remarkable centurion is a model of prayer. This man's faith in Jesus brought amazement and touched his heart. We too can touch the heart of Jesus when we pray with deep concern for someone in need.

• Who are the people in my life who need prayer? How might I bring their needs to Jesus?

Tuesday 5th December
Luke 10:21–24

At that same hour Jesus rejoiced in the Holy Spirit and said, "I thank you, Father, Lord of heaven and earth, because you have hidden these things from the wise and the intelligent and have revealed them to infants; yes, Father, for such was your gracious will. All things have been handed over to me by my Father;

and no one knows who the Son is except the Father, or who the Father is except the Son and anyone to whom the Son chooses to reveal him."

Then turning to the disciples, Jesus said to them privately, "Blessed are the eyes that see what you see! For I tell you that many prophets and kings desired to see what you see, but did not see it, and to hear what you hear, but did not hear it."

- This lovely prayer of Jesus tells us something of the relationship he treasured with his Father through the Holy Spirit. It is his prayer of thanksgiving for the successful mission of his disciples, whom he had sent out to preach. Jesus then tells them that they are indeed blessed to have accepted the good news and to be building their lives on their relationship with God.

- Let us pray that, like the disciples, we have the "eyes to see and the ears to hear."

Wednesday 6th December
Matthew 15:29–37

After Jesus had left that place, he passed along the Sea of Galilee, and he went up the mountain, where he sat down. Great crowds came to him, bringing with them the lame, the maimed, the blind, the mute, and many others. They put them at his feet, and he cured them, so that the crowd was amazed when they saw the mute speaking, the maimed whole, the lame walking, and the blind seeing. And they praised the God of Israel. Then Jesus called his disciples to him and said, "I have compassion for the crowd, because they have been with me now for three days and have nothing to eat; and I do not want to send them away hungry, for they might faint on the way." The disciples said to him, "Where are we to get enough bread in the desert to feed so great a crowd?" Jesus asked them, "How many loaves have you?" They said, "Seven, and a few small fish." Then ordering the crowd to sit down on the ground, he took the seven loaves and the fish; and after giving thanks he broke them and gave them to the disciples, and the disciples gave them to the crowds. And all of them ate and were filled; and they took up the broken pieces left over, seven baskets full.

- Lord, you are the one who notices when we are hungry, tired, or disorganized, and without making a fuss you reach out to our needs. The crowds wore you out, bringing you the maimed, the mute, and the blind. Again and again in the Gospels, you are the one who feeds the hungry and gives them strength for their journey. You are the bread of life.

- What resources do I have that, today, Jesus might use to help others?

Thursday 7th December
Matthew 7:21, 24–27

[Jesus said to the people,] "Not everyone who says to me, 'Lord, Lord,' will enter the kingdom of heaven, but only one who does the will of my Father in heaven. . . . Everyone then who hears these words of mine and acts on them will be like a wise man who built his house on rock. The rain fell, the floods came, and the winds blew and beat on that house, but it did not fall, because it had been founded on rock. And everyone who hears these words of mine and does not act on them will be like a foolish man who built his house on sand. The rain fell, and the floods came, and the winds blew and beat against that house, and it fell—and great was its fall!"

• The Lord is the everlasting rock, says the prophet Isaiah, so trust in the Lord forever. "For he has brought low the inhabitants of the height; the lofty city he lays low." . . . But the faithful ones, on the other hand, can say, "he sets up victory like walls and bulwarks . . . we have a strong city" (Isaiah 26). Any moment now, he's going to come and surround us with protection.

• It is the Lord who is "the rock of ages"—a still point, though the centuries swirl around. The Lord is a solid center on which we can build our life. If we are faithful to the Lord, the Lord is faithful to us.

Friday 8th December
The Immaculate Conception of
the Blessed Virgin Mary
Luke 1:26–38

In the sixth month the angel Gabriel was sent by God to a town in Galilee called Nazareth, to a virgin engaged to a man whose name was Joseph, of the house of David. The virgin's name was Mary. And he came to her and said, "Greetings, favored one! The Lord is with you." But she was much perplexed by his words and pondered what sort of greeting this might be. The angel said to her, "Do not be afraid, Mary, for you have found favor with God. And now, you will conceive in your womb and bear a son, and you will name him Jesus. He will be great, and will be called the Son of the Most High, and the Lord God will give to him the throne of his ancestor David. He will reign over the house of Jacob forever, and of his kingdom there will be no end." Mary said to the angel, "How can this be, since I am a virgin?" The angel said to her, "The Holy Spirit will come upon you, and the power of the Most High will overshadow you; therefore the child to be born will be holy; he will be called Son of God. And now, your relative Elizabeth in her old age has also conceived a son; and this is the sixth month for her who was said to be barren. For nothing will be impossible with God." Then Mary said, "Here am I, the servant of the Lord; let it be with me according to your word." Then the angel departed from her.

- Scripture leaves us in no doubt about God being a long-range planner; he can determine that a whole series of events come to maturity in his own good time. In fact, he has done this for the benefit of us all—planning, even before the beginning of the world, for us to become sisters and brothers of Jesus.

- For the grand plan to come to completion, the co-operation of Mary was needed. God still asks for our cooperation in the overall plan of his kingdom here on earth. Where do I fit in that plan today, or this week?

Saturday 9th December
Matthew 9:35—10:1, 5a, 6–8

Then Jesus went about all the cities and villages, teaching in their synagogues, and proclaiming the good news of the kingdom, and curing every disease and every sickness. When he saw the crowds, he had compassion for them, because they were harassed and helpless, like sheep without a shepherd. Then he said to his disciples, "The harvest is plentiful, but the laborers are few; therefore, ask the Lord of the harvest to send out laborers into his harvest." Then Jesus summoned his twelve disciples and gave them authority over unclean spirits, to cast them out, and to cure every disease and every sickness. These twelve Jesus sent out with the following instructions: "Go nowhere among the Gentiles, and enter no town of the Samaritans, but go rather to the lost sheep of the house of Israel. As you go, proclaim the good news, 'The kingdom of heaven has come near.' Cure the sick, raise the dead, cleanse the lepers, cast out demons. You received without payment; give without payment."

- The Twelve are to perform cures, to cast out devils—and even to raise the dead. (All in the day's work, as it were.) Indeed, something totally new must be stirring!

- A shepherd-king has suddenly arrived: Jesus, full of compassion, is bringing heaven close to earth. I have the power, through the Holy Spirit, to express that compassion in my situations and relationships this very day.

The Second Week of Advent
December 10—December 16, 2017

Something to think and pray about each day this week:

Signs of the Savior
When I was in my early twenties, I backpacked around Scotland. At my northernmost destination, I stayed at a sheep farm. I remember waking up in the middle of the night, checking my watch, only four o'clock, and being shocked to see the sun outside my window blazing down on the fields. Since I'd expected darkness, the sun seemed unbearably bright. Later, on the Isle of Skye, I watched the sun go down at ten at night and the sky gradually grow a darker blue but never turn black. I'm sure the natives barely noticed, but to me this perpetual daylight seemed like a sign. Though we sometimes turn away from brightness, preferring dark, the light is out there burning always, pouring through the universe at the greatest possible speed, forever coming, light upon light, dawning through the darkness.

—Amy Andrews, *2017: A Book of Grace-Filled Days*

The Presence of God

"Come to me, all you who are weary and are carrying heavy burdens, and I will give you rest." Here I am, Lord. I come to seek your presence. I long for your healing power.

Freedom

"In these days, God taught me as a schoolteacher teaches a pupil" (Saint Ignatius).
I remind myself that there are things God has to teach me yet, and I ask for the grace to hear those things and let them change me.

Consciousness

Help me, Lord, to be more conscious of your presence. Teach me to recognize your presence in others. Fill my heart with gratitude for the times your love has been shown to me through the care of others.

The Word

God speaks to each of us individually. I listen attentively, to hear what he is saying to me. Read the text a few times, then listen. (Please turn to the Scripture on the following pages. Inspiration points are there should you need them. When you are ready, return here to continue.)

Conversation

Conversation requires talking and listening.

As I talk to Jesus, may I also learn to be still and listen.

I picture the gentleness in his eyes and the smile full of love as he gazes on me.

I can be totally honest with Jesus as I tell him of my worries and my cares.

I will open my heart to him as I tell him of my fears and my doubts.

I will ask him to help me place myself fully in his care and to abandon myself to him, knowing that he always wants what is best for me.

Conclusion

I thank God for these moments we have spent together and for any insights I have been given concerning the text.

Sunday 10th December
Second Sunday of Advent
Mark 1:1–8

The beginning of the good news of Jesus Christ, the Son of God.

As it is written by the prophet Isaiah,

"See, I am sending my messenger ahead of you,
    who will prepare your way;
the voice of one crying out in the wilderness:
    'Prepare the way of the Lord,
    make his paths straight,'"

John the baptizer appeared in the wilderness, proclaiming a baptism of repentance for the forgiveness of sins. And people from the whole Judean countryside and all the people of Jerusalem were going out to him, and were baptized by him in the river Jordan, confessing their sins. Now John was clothed with camel's hair, with a leather belt around his waist, and he ate locusts and wild honey. He proclaimed, "The one who is more powerful than I is coming after me; I am not worthy to stoop down and untie the thong of his sandals. I have baptized you with water; but he will baptize you with the Holy Spirit."

- Imagine yourself witnessing this scene, perhaps standing in the shallows with the water flowing around your ankles. Allow the scene to unfold. What is it like? The young man from Nazareth joins those waiting for John's baptism: a symbol of purification but also of birth—coming up out of the waters of the womb into a new life as God's beloved child.

• Lord, when I realize that you love me, it is like the start of a new life. As I hear your voice, I know that I have a purpose and a destiny.

Monday 11th December
Luke 5:17–26

One day, while he was teaching, Pharisees and teachers of the law were sitting nearby (they had come from every village of Galilee and Judea and from Jerusalem); and the power of the Lord was with him to heal. Just then some men came, carrying a paralyzed man on a bed. They were trying to bring him in and lay him before Jesus; but finding no way to bring him in because of the crowd, they went up on the roof and let him down with his bed through the tiles into the middle of the crowd in front of Jesus. When he saw their faith, he said, "Friend, your sins are forgiven you." Then the scribes and the Pharisees began to question, "Who is this who is speaking blasphemies? Who can forgive sins but God alone?" When Jesus perceived their questionings, he answered them,

"Why do you raise such questions in your hearts? Which is easier, to say, 'Your sins are forgiven you,' or to say, 'Stand up and walk'? But so that you may know that the Son of Man has authority on earth to forgive sins"—he said to the one who was para-lyzed—"I say to you, stand up and take your bed and go to your home." Immediately he stood up before them, took what he had been lying on, and went to his home, glorifying God. Amazement seized all of them, and they glorified God and were filled with awe, saying, "We have seen strange things today."

- Jesus is the newly arrived kingdom, personified in his very self. Not only has he power to cure the paralyzed man, he also lays claim to forgive the man's sins—and this requires nothing less than God's own power.

- "We have seen strange things today," say the on-lookers. Nothing had prepared them for this. But this precisely is what our Advent season is about. We are commemorating the first coming of a Savior, and we are also preparing a welcome for this Savior in our own hearts and in the world of today.

Tuesday 12th December
Luke 1:39–47

In those days Mary set out and went with haste to a Judean town in the hill country, where she entered the house of Zechariah and greeted Elizabeth. When Elizabeth heard Mary's greeting, the child leapt in her womb. And Elizabeth was filled with the Holy Spirit and exclaimed with a loud cry, "Blessed are you among women, and blessed is the fruit of your womb. And why has this happened to me, that the mother of my Lord comes to me? For as soon as I heard the sound of your greeting, the child in my womb leapt for joy. And blessed is she who believed that there would be a fulfillment of what was spoken to her by the Lord."

And Mary said,

"My soul magnifies the Lord,
    and my spirit rejoices in God my Savior."

- I marvel at the instincts and insight of mothers. While husband Zechariah is baffled and struck dumb and foster-father Joseph has misgivings, it is a woman, Elizabeth, herself pregnant, who recognizes the action of the Lord in her young cousin. She is given the special grace of an intimate appreciation of what is happening and who is really present.

- In daily life, do I always appreciate what is happening and who is really present?

Wednesday 13th December
Matthew 11:28–30

[Jesus said,] "Come to me, all you that are weary and are carrying heavy burdens, and I will give you rest. Take my yoke upon you, and learn from me; for I am gentle and humble in heart, and you will find rest for your souls. For my yoke is easy, and my burden is light."

• The reign of the coming Savior king will not just bring security and welcome to anyone who feels lost and abandoned. Jesus' kingdom also promises relief and support to those who simply feel that life has become too much for them.

• Jesus understands each of us better than we understand ourselves. His heart, gentle and humble, goes out to us. What burdens of mine does he offer to help me with today?

Thursday 14th December
Matthew 11:11–15

Jesus said, "Truly I tell you, among those born of women no one has arisen greater than John the Baptist; yet the least in the kingdom of heaven is greater than he. From the days of John the Baptist until now the kingdom of heaven has suffered violence, and the violent take it by force. For all the prophets and the law prophesied until John came;

and if you are willing to accept it, he is Elijah who is to come. Let anyone with ears listen!"

- What was it that placed John the Baptist below the least in the kingdom of heaven? He had preached the justice of God and the need for repentance; but he had not lived to see Jesus crucified and, in that, to see the unbelievable extent of God's love for us.

- "If you are willing to accept it, he is Elijah . . ." Has God revealed anything to me lately that I felt unwilling to accept? When do we know that we are willing, or not willing, to receive God's revelation?

Friday 15th December
Matthew 11:16–19

[Jesus spoke to the crowds,] "But to what will I compare this generation? It is like children sitting in the marketplaces and calling to one another,

'We played the flute for you, and you did not
   dance;
we wailed, and you did not mourn.'

For John came neither eating nor drinking, and they say, 'He has a demon'; the Son of Man came eating and drinking, and they say, 'Look, a glutton and a drunkard, a friend of tax collectors and sinners!' Yet wisdom is vindicated by her deeds."

- The Lord has always wanted to shower his people with gifts. But often when the offer was made (through the mouth of his messengers, the prophets), the people turned their backs. In fact, even as Jesus prepared to begin his public ministry, this was still happening. The people refused the message of John the Baptist; it was no surprise that Jesus himself met opposition.

- Jesus has arrived offering the gift of new life in abundance, but we remain choosy about the way his message comes to us; it is "too churchy" on the one hand or "too worldly" on the other. May we pray during this season that our hearts become more open.

Saturday 16th December
Matthew 17:9a, 10–13

As they were coming down the mountain, Jesus ordered them, "Tell no one about the vision until after the Son of Man has been raised from the dead." And the disciples asked him, "Why, then, do the scribes say that Elijah must come first?" He replied, "Elijah is indeed coming and will restore all things; but I tell you that Elijah has already come, and they did not recognize him, but they did to him whatever they pleased. So also the Son of Man is about to suffer at their hands." Then the disciples understood that he was speaking to them about John the Baptist.

- The Jewish faith looked forward to the "last days" or end time, when the Lord would come in glory and finally wrap up the affairs of this world. And a conviction had arisen that the approach of the end time would be signaled by a forerunner; the figure of the larger-than-life prophet Elijah would make a renewed appearance. The coming of Jesus was meant to bring about the kingdom of God on earth with the offer of salvation for all, but the people struck out against the bearer of the message.

- By our prayer this Christmas, we can ensure that the newly born Jesus is welcome in our lives, even if his message turns some of our values on their heads.

December 17—December 23, 2017

Something to think and pray about each day this week:

Preparing Our Hearts

The great purge of every nook and cranny of our home has begun. We are in the process of sharing our toys, outgrown clothes, and superfluous belongings. We are letting go of the things we have held onto "just in case" and other things that have cluttered our lives just because we haven't had the time to clear things out on a regular basis. The resulting space that we are recovering in our home is freeing. There is more room to move and more room to live. There is more space to focus on the things that really matter—and those things are *not things*.

As we clear the clutter from our home, I am reminded that Advent is a great time to clear the spiritual clutter as well. I ask myself, when Jesus comes, will there be room for him to stay, or will he find my heart and soul too cluttered? Am I hanging onto things I don't need out of that "just in case" type of fear? Or, do I trust him enough to let everything go? Have I taken the necessary time to free up space for him? Is my priority, in fact, Jesus, or is it things or other attachments? When he comes, will I be able to respond to him freely, or will my movements be impeded by stuff that's holding me back? My soul-cleaning goal is to be able to fling open the door to my heart and fearlessly let go of all of those things that might get in the way of his entry. Can I do this?

—Rebecca Ruiz on *dotMagis*,
the blog of *IgnatianSpirituality.com*

The Presence of God

"I am standing at the door, knocking," says the Lord. What a wonderful privilege that the Lord of all creation desires to come to me. I welcome his presence.

Freedom

Leave me here freely all alone / In cell where never sunlight shone / should no one ever speak to me. / This golden silence makes me free.

—Part of a poem written by a prisoner at
Dachau concentration camp

Consciousness

How am I really feeling? Lighthearted? Heavyhearted? I may be very much at peace, happy to be here. Equally, I may be frustrated, worried, or angry. I acknowledge how I really am. It is the real me whom the Lord loves.

The Word

I take my time to read the word of God, slowly, a few times, allowing myself to dwell on anything that strikes me. (Please turn to the Scripture on the following pages. Inspiration points are there should you need them. When you are ready, return here to continue.)

Conversation

Do I notice myself reacting as I pray with the word of God? Do I feel challenged, comforted, angry? Imagining Jesus sitting or standing by me, I speak out my feelings, as one trusted friend to another.

Conclusion

Glory be to the Father, and to the Son, and to the Holy Spirit,
As it was in the beginning, is now and ever shall be,
World without end. Amen.

Sunday 17th December
Third Sunday of Advent
John 1:6–8, 19–28

There was a man sent from God, whose name was John. He came as a witness to testify to the light, so that all might believe through him. He himself was not the light, but he came to testify to the light. . . . This is the testimony given by John when the Jews sent priests and Levites from Jerusalem to ask him, "Who are you?" He confessed and did not deny it, but confessed, "I am not the Messiah." And they asked him, "What then? Are you Elijah?" He said, "I am not." "Are you the prophet?" He answered, "No." Then they said to him, "Who are you? Let us have an answer for those who sent us. What do you say about yourself?" He said,

"I am the voice of one crying out in the wilderness,
'Make straight the way of the Lord,'"
as the prophet Isaiah said.

Now they had been sent from the Pharisees. They asked him, "Why then are you baptizing if you are neither the Messiah, nor Elijah, nor the prophet?" John answered them, "I baptize with water. Among you stands one whom you do not know, the one who is coming after me; I am not worthy to untie the thong of his sandal." This took place in Bethany across the Jordan where John was baptizing.

- Here are questions we can ask about ourselves: Who am I? What is my purpose in God's scheme?

- Lord, I think of you beside me, seeing the good and the promise in me. This is what I want to say about myself: I am called into being by God, who loves me.

Monday 18th December
Matthew 1:18–25

Now the birth of Jesus the Messiah took place in this way. When his mother Mary had been engaged to Joseph, but before they lived together, she was found to be with child from the Holy Spirit. Her husband Joseph, being a righteous man and unwilling to expose her to public disgrace, planned to dismiss her quietly. But just when he had resolved to do this, an angel of the Lord appeared to him in a dream and said, "Joseph, son of David, do not be afraid to take Mary as your wife, for the child conceived in her is from the Holy Spirit. She will bear a son, and you are to name him Jesus, for he will save his people from their sins." All this took place to fulfill what had been spoken by the Lord through the prophet:

"Look, the virgin shall conceive and bear a son,
    and they shall name him Emmanuel,"

which means, "God is with us." When Joseph awoke from sleep, he did as the angel of the Lord commanded him; he took her as his wife, but had no marital relations with her until she had borne a son; and he named him Jesus.

- Jean Paul Sartre, philosopher and atheist, once wrote a Christmas play, *Bariona*. In it he tries to imagine Joseph in Bethlehem: "He [Joseph] feels himself slightly out of it. He suffers because he sees how much this woman whom he loves resembles God; how she is already at the side of God. For God has burst like a bomb into the intimacy of this family. Joseph and Mary are separated forever by this explosion of light. And I imagine that all through his life Joseph will be learning to accept this."

- There is a model here for making decisions and dealing with doubts. Pray about it, carry it as a question, pester God about it. This is the story of Joseph's utterly unique vocation, as foster-father of the Son of God.

Tuesday 19th December

Luke 1:5–25

In the days of King Herod of Judea, there was a priest named Zechariah, who belonged to the priestly order of Abijah. His wife was a descendant of Aaron, and her name was Elizabeth. Both of them were righteous before God, living blamelessly according to all the commandments and regulations of the Lord. But they had no children, because Elizabeth was barren, and both were getting on in years. Once when he was serving as priest before God and his section was on duty, he was chosen by lot, according to the custom of the priesthood, to enter the sanctuary of the Lord and offer incense. Now at the time of the incense of-fering, the whole assembly of the people was praying outside. Then there appeared to him an angel of the Lord, standing at the right side of the altar of incense. When Zechariah saw him, he was terrified; and fear overwhelmed him. But the angel said to him, "Do not be afraid, Zechariah, for your prayer has been heard. Your wife Elizabeth will bear you a son, and you will name him John. You will have joy and glad-ness, and many will rejoice at his birth, for he will be great in the sight of the Lord. He must never drink wine or strong drink; even before his birth he will be filled with the Holy Spirit. He will turn many of the people of Israel to the Lord their God. With the spirit and power of Elijah he will go before him, to turn the hearts of parents to their children, and the disobedient to the wisdom of the righteous, to make ready a people prepared for the Lord." Zechariah said to the angel, "How will I know that this is so? For I am an old man, and my wife is getting on in years." The angel replied, "I am Gabriel. I stand in the presence of God, and I have been sent to speak to you and to bring you this good news. But now, because you did not believe my words, which will be fulfilled in their time, you will become mute, unable to speak, until the day these things occur." Meanwhile the people were waiting for Zechariah, and wondered at his delay in the sanctuary. When he did come out, he could not speak to them, and they realized that he had seen a vision in the sanctuary. He kept motioning to them and remained unable to speak. When his time of service was ended, he went to his home.

After those days his wife Elizabeth conceived, and for five months she remained in seclusion. She said, "This is what the Lord has done for me when he looked favorably on me and took away the disgrace I have endured among my people."

- On the basis of their faithfulness to God, Zechariah and Elizabeth could be rated as being "one in a thousand." But, to the external view, both were unknown and just like a thousand others. Harder still, they were childless, which was seen in those days to indicate the absence of God's favor. But they were already in God's plan for the world's coming Savior.

- Certainly, God's ways are not our ways, and the very people who have tried to remain fully loyal to the Lord are sometimes going to find themselves called to deeper faith—involving an ever more privileged closeness to God. We might ask, in what ways is my faith being called upon to grow?

Wednesday 20 December
Luke 1:26–38

In the sixth month the angel Gabriel was sent by God to a town in Galilee called Nazareth, to a virgin engaged to a man whose name was Joseph, of the house of David. The virgin's name was Mary. And he came to her and said, "Greetings, favored one! The Lord is with you." But she was much perplexed by his words and pondered what sort of greeting this might be. The angel said to her, "Do not be afraid, Mary, for you have found favor with God. And now, you will conceive in your womb and bear a son, and you will name him Jesus. He will be great, and will be called the Son of the Most High, and the Lord God will give to him the throne of his ancestor David. He will reign over the house of Jacob forever, and of his kingdom there will be no end." Mary said to the angel, "How can this be, since I am a virgin?" The angel said to her, "The Holy Spirit will come upon you, and the power of the Most High will overshadow you; therefore the child to be born will be holy; he will be called Son of God. And now, your relative Elizabeth in her old age has also conceived a son; and this is the sixth month for her who was said to be barren. For nothing will be impossible with God." Then Mary said, "Here am I, the servant of the Lord; let it be with me according to your word." Then the angel departed from her.

- For any young woman of Israel, the gift of a child—fruitfulness—was a special mark of God's favor. But before Mary even has time to take in this news, she is confronted by the announcement that her future son will be "savior" (the meaning of *Jesus*)—successor to the kingship of David—Son of the Most High. Still trying to come to terms with it all, imagine her consternation as she realizes that not even a first step is in place; she is as yet no more than betrothed. Then the announcing angel compounds her wonder by speaking of God's action in bestowing a son on the aged Elizabeth.

- Is there such a thing as being overwhelmed with good news? It appears that this was the case with the young, yet willing, Mary. Am I willing to be overwhelmed by the potential God has placed in my life?

Thursday 21st December
Luke 1:39–45

In those days Mary set out and went with haste to a Judean town in the hill country, where she entered the house of Zechariah and greeted Elizabeth. When Elizabeth heard Mary's greeting, the child leaped in her womb. And Elizabeth was filled with the Holy Spirit and exclaimed with a loud cry, "Blessed are you among women, and blessed is the fruit of your womb. And why has this happened to me, that the mother of my Lord comes to me? For as soon as I heard the sound of your greeting, the child in my womb leaped for joy. And blessed is she who believed that there would be a fulfillment of what was spoken to her by the Lord."

- Jesus, the child that Mary is carrying, is recognized by the child in Elizabeth's womb; John leaps in recognition of the one both mothers revere as "Lord" (John himself being of miraculous origin from an elderly mother). Not only is this a confirmation for both women, but their miraculous situations bring them together in a special sort of faith community.

- And above and beyond what is happening to each mother, the Lord (long awaited) has finally come to visit his people, to be victorious over enemies, to exult with joy over those who are his own. We can rest in the confidence that our individual stories are always part of a larger, eternal story.

Friday 22nd December
Luke 1:46–56

And Mary said,

"My soul magnifies the Lord,
      and my spirit rejoices in God my Savior,
for he has looked with favor on the lowliness of his
            servant.
      Surely, from now on all generations will call me
            blessed;
for the Mighty One has done great things for me,
      and holy is his name.
His mercy is for those who fear him from generation
      to generation.
He has shown strength with his arm;
      he has scattered the proud in the thoughts of
      their hearts.
He has brought down the powerful from their
            thrones,
      and lifted up the lowly;

he has filled the hungry with good things,
    and sent the rich away empty.
He has helped his servant Israel,
    in remembrance of his mercy,
according to the promise he made to our ancestors,
    to Abraham and to his descendants forever."

And Mary remained with [Elizabeth] about three
months and then returned to her home.

- Although Mary is giving thanks for the honor
  accorded her, this is a self-effacing prayer. It is a
  hymn of praise for everything the Lord has done
  for his people—the people as a whole (descendants
  of Abraham)—as well as anyone anywhere who
  truly reveres [fears] God. There is joy and exulta-
  tion which the angels around Bethlehem will also
  give voice to at the coming of salvation.

- As I look at my life this day, what blessings do I
  see? And how do my personal blessings connect
  with what God is doing for the whole world?

Saturday 23rd December
Luke 1:57–66

Now the time came for Elizabeth to give birth, and
she bore a son. Her neighbors and relatives heard that
the Lord had shown his great mercy to her, and they
rejoiced with her.

On the eighth day they came to circumcise the child, and they were going to name him Zechariah after his father. But his mother said, "No; he is to be called John." They said to her, "None of your relatives has this name." Then they began motioning to his father to find out what name he wanted to give him. He asked for a writing tablet and wrote, "His name is John." And all of them were amazed. Immediately his mouth was opened and his tongue freed, and he began to speak, praising God. Fear came over all their neighbors, and all these things were talked about throughout the entire hill country of Judea. All who heard them pondered them and said, "What then will this child become?" For, indeed, the hand of the Lord was with him.

- Zechariah and Elizabeth have been blessed with this new life in their declining years. And through the miracle of the unexpected birth—and of the binding and loosing of Zechariah's tongue—the people realize that here God is taking a very direct hand in events. They know that they are on the threshold of mystery.

- My life, too, is reason for rejoicing because God has planted within it a purpose that is unique to my situation, my history, and my gifts. May I thank God for all of this and offer it back to him.

December 24—December 30, 2017

Something to think and pray about each day this week:

What Are We Expecting?

I don't believe that Christianity is a departure from all that came before. I don't believe, in some sense, that there is anything new under the sun. And yet the birth of Jesus changed everything. Before he came, there was a great yearning expressed in the myths, in philosophy, in the words of the prophets. These voices cried out their hope that God would not abandon us to death, that there was meaning beyond life. On Christmas Day the life that would answer these voices was again made visible. It came not as a new thing but as a confirmation, a proclamation that what had long been hoped for, theorized, prophesied now lay under the sun as real as you and I.

—Amy Andrews, *2017: A Book of Grace-Filled Days*

The Presence of God

"Be still, and know that I am God!" Lord, may your spirit guide me to seek your loving presence more and more for it is there I find rest and refreshment from this busy world.

Freedom

By God's grace I was born to live in freedom. Free to enjoy the pleasures he created for me. Dear Lord, grant that I may live as you intended, with complete confidence in your loving care.

Consciousness

How am I today?

Where am I with God? With others?

Do I have something to be grateful for? Then I give thanks.

Is there something I am sorry for? Then I ask forgiveness.

The Word

God speaks to each of us individually. I need to listen, to hear what he is saying to me. Read the text a few times, then listen. (Please turn to the Scripture on the following pages. Inspiration points are there should you need them. When you are ready, return here to continue.)

Conversation
How has God's word moved me? Has it left me cold?
Has it consoled me or moved me to act in a new way?
I imagine Jesus standing or sitting beside me.
I turn and share my feelings with him.

Conclusion
I thank God for these moments we have spent together and for any insights I have been given concerning
the text.

Sunday 24th December
Fourth Sunday of Advent
Luke 1:26–38

In the sixth month the angel Gabriel was sent by God to a town in Galilee called Nazareth, to a virgin engaged to a man whose name was Joseph, of the house of David. The virgin's name was Mary. And he came to her and said, "Greetings, favored one! The Lord is with you." But she was much perplexed by his words and pondered what sort of greeting this might be. The angel said to her, "Do not be afraid, Mary, for you have found favor with God. And now, you will conceive in your womb and bear a son, and you will name him Jesus. He will be great, and will be called the Son of the Most High, and the Lord God will give to him the throne of his ancestor David. He will reign over the house of Jacob forever, and of his kingdom there will be no end." Mary said to the angel, "How can this be, since I am a virgin?" The angel said to her, "The Holy Spirit will come upon you, and the power of the Most High will overshadow you; therefore the child to be born will be holy; he will be called Son of God. And now, your relative Elizabeth in her old age has also conceived a son; and this is the sixth month for her who was said to be barren. For nothing will be impossible with God." Then Mary said, "Here am I, the servant of the Lord; let it be with me according to your word." Then the angel departed from her.

- When a woman in the crowd cried to Jesus, "Blessed is the womb that bore you," he replied, "Blessed rather are those who hear the word of God and obey it." The first of these was his mother, who said "Let it be with me according to your word." We remember her words whenever we pray the Angelus.

- Lord, this is not an easy prayer to make. You prayed it yourself in Gethsemane in a sweat of blood, "not my will but yours be done." Help me make it the pattern of my life. What issues of surrender and trust does it raise for me?

Monday 25th December
The Nativity of the Lord (Christmas)
John 1:1–18

In the beginning was the Word, and the Word was with God, and the Word was God. He was in the beginning with God. All things came into being through him, and without him not one thing came into being. What has come into being in him was life, and the life was the light of all people. The light shines in the darkness, and the darkness did not overcome it.

There was a man sent from God, whose name was John. He came as a witness to testify to the light, so that all might believe through him. He himself was not the light, but he came to testify to the light. The true light, which enlightens everyone, was coming into the world.

He was in the world, and the world came into being through him; yet the world did not know him. He came to what was his own, and his own people did not accept him. But to all who received him, who believed in his name, he gave power to become children of God, who were born, not of blood or of the will of the flesh or of the will of man, but of God.

And the Word became flesh and lived among us, and we have seen his glory, the glory as of a father's only son, full of grace and truth. (John testified to him and cried out, "This was he of whom I said, 'He who comes after me ranks ahead of me because he was before me.'") From his fullness we have all received, grace upon grace. The law indeed was given through Moses; grace and truth came through Jesus Christ. No one has ever seen God. It is God the only Son, who is close to the Father's heart, who has made him known.

- In this hymn, which introduces the fourth Gospel, John proclaims the faith that marks us as Christians. We believe that Jesus is the word of

God, his perfect expression. "No one has ever seen God. It is God the only Son, who is close to the Father's heart, who has made him known."

- Lord, in the year that starts tonight, let me grow in the knowledge of God. May I receive of your fullness, grace upon grace. You took on this mortal flesh for me and lived among us. May this coming year bring me closer to you.

Tuesday 26th December
Matthew 10:17–22

Beware of them, for they will hand you over to councils and flog you in their synagogues; and you will be dragged before governors and kings because of me, as a testimony to them and the Gentiles. When they hand you over, do not worry about how you are to speak or what you are to say; for what you are to say will be given to you at that time; for it is not you who speak, but the Spirit of your Father speaking through you. Brother will betray brother to death, and a father his child, and children will rise against parents and have them put to death; and you will be hated by all because of my name. But the one who endures to the end will be saved.

- Jesus gave up heaven's glory to join our life on earth. And the Christian, in turn, often must give up earth's privileges, even the freedom to live, to be worthy of joining the life of heaven. Martyrdom happened to Stephen, and we cannot rule out its happening to any of us.

- How often do I expect special privileges in this life because I'm a Christian? When have I needed to give up privilege to live as God asked me to live?

Wednesday 27th December
John 20:1a, 2–8

Early on the first day of the week, while it was still dark, Mary Magdalene came to the tomb and saw that the stone had been removed from the tomb.

So she ran and went to Simon Peter and the other disciple, the one whom Jesus loved, and said to them, "They have taken the Lord out of the tomb, and we do not know where they have laid him." Then Peter and the other disciple set out and went towards the tomb. The two were running together, but the other disciple outran Peter and reached the tomb first. He bent down to look in and saw the linen wrappings lying there, but he did not go in. Then Simon Peter came, following him, and went into the tomb. He saw the linen wrappings lying there, and the cloth that had been on Jesus' head, not lying with the linen wrappings but rolled up in a place by itself. Then the other disciple, who reached the tomb first, also went in, and he saw and believed.

- It may be unfair to say that one person is "better" at believing than another; but today's Gospel passage gives us a portrait of two followers of Jesus. The strong point of one of them (Peter) is, you might say, action; and the strong point of the other (the apostle John, today's saint) is believing. Perhaps that's why John—seemingly more attuned to the inner sense of things—is called "the one whom Jesus loved."

- In the words of one Gospel petitioner, we say, "I believe; Help my unbelief!" I give myself permission to pray this prayer. The praying itself will prepare my life for more faith.

Thursday 28th December
Matthew 2:13–18

Now after they had left, an angel of the Lord appeared to Joseph in a dream and said, "Get up, take the child and his mother, and flee to Egypt, and remain there until I tell you; for Herod is about to search for the child, to destroy him." Then Joseph got up, took the child and his mother by night, and went to Egypt, and remained there until the death of Herod. This was to fulfill what had been spoken by the Lord through the prophet, "Out of Egypt I have called my son."

When Herod saw that he had been tricked by the wise men, he was infuriated, and he sent and killed all the children in and around Bethlehem who were two years old or under, according to the time that he had learned from the wise men. Then was fulfilled what had been spoken through the prophet Jeremiah:

"A voice was heard in Ramah,
  wailing and loud lamentation,
Rachel weeping for her children;
  she refused to be consoled, because they are no
    more."

- When we reflect on the scene of the Holy Family forced to flee into Egypt, we remember the Jewish people once found themselves in captivity in Egypt. They were eventually released by the Pharaoh after the blood of a child flowed in every house of his people.

- Mothers who are separated from their children by death or exile will mourn continuously. I pray for those families, that they will find comfort in the ever-present compassion of God.

Friday 29th December
Luke 2:22–35

When the time came for their purification according to the law of Moses, they brought him up to

Jerusalem to present him to the Lord (as it is written in the law of the Lord, "Every firstborn male shall be designated as holy to the Lord"), and they offered a sacrifice according to what is stated in the law of the Lord, "a pair of turtledoves or two young pigeons."

Now there was a man in Jerusalem whose name was Simeon; this man was righteous and devout, looking forward to the consolation of Israel, and the Holy Spirit rested on him. It had been revealed to him by the Holy Spirit that he would not see death before he had seen the Lord's Messiah. Guided by the Spirit, Simeon came into the temple; and when the parents brought in the child Jesus, to do for him what was customary under the law, Simeon took him in his arms and praised God, saying,

"Master, now you are dismissing your servant in
         peace,
     according to your word;
for my eyes have seen your salvation,
     which you have prepared in the presence of all
         peoples,
a light for revelation to the Gentiles
     and for glory to your people Israel."

And the child's father and mother were amazed at what was being said about him. Then Simeon blessed them and said to his mother Mary, "This child is destined for the falling and the rising of many in Israel, and to be a sign that will be opposed so that the inner thoughts of many will be revealed—and a sword will pierce your own soul too."

• The Scripture readings in the season of Christmas often emphasize how the coming of Jesus was the end point of all the initiatives God had taken in the interests of the people he had chosen. And today we're reminded that this was true for the whole non-Jewish world as well. But we are warned not to be complacent. Jesus is not going to force himself on anybody. There will always be the choice to accept him or to reject him.

• In my prayer today, I rely on the Holy Spirit to help me as I make choices. I have a destiny too, but God honors my ability to say yes or no.

Saturday 30th December
Luke 2:36–40

There was also a prophet, Anna the daughter of Phanuel, of the tribe of Asher. She was of a great age, having lived with her husband seven years after her marriage, then as a widow to the age of eighty-four. She never left the temple but worshipped there with fasting and prayer night and day. At that moment she came, and began to praise God and to speak about the child to all who were looking for the redemption of Jerusalem.

When they had finished everything required by the law of the Lord, they returned to Galilee, to their own town of Nazareth. The child grew and became strong, filled with wisdom; and the favor of God was upon him.

- As Anna took the baby in her arms and her eyes lit up, how Mary must have warmed to her! Here was yet another confirmation of this child's destiny as the chosen one. Mary had no way of knowing that Anna had waited many years to see this one child. Anna did not know who the child would be—or who the child's parents would be—until they appeared that day. Yet all were ready to see God's revelation when it appeared.

- Lord, you are telling me that I don't have to know the details of how your grace will come about in my life. I need only to be ready to recognize it when the time comes.

First Week of Christmas/Epiphany of Our Lord
December 31, 2017—January 7, 2018

Something to think and pray about each day this week:

True Gift Giving

There are countless stories and legends about the deeds of St. Nicholas, a bishop of Myra in what's now Turkey, back in the fourth century. I suppose the most well-known story is that of the dowry. A man was too poor to provide dowries for his daughters, so Bishop Nicholas found ways to get the needed funds to the family, in secret. The thing I like about the story is that Nicholas was so determined to be anonymous in his giving that, for the last daughter, he supposedly dropped the bag of cash down the chimney. It gives me something to think about. In this season of gift giving, is my heart truly centered on others, or do I give in order to impress?

—Amy Welborn, *A Catholic Woman's Book of Days*

The Presence of God
As I sit here, the beating of my heart,
the ebb and flow of my breathing, the movements of
my mind
are all signs of God's ongoing creation of me.
I pause for a moment and become aware
of this presence of God within me.

Freedom
Everything has the potential to draw from me a fuller
love and life.
Yet my desires are often fixed, caught, on illusions of
fulfillment.
I ask that God, through my freedom, may orches-
trate my desires in a vibrant loving melody rich in
harmony.

Consciousness
I ask, how am I within myself today? Am I particularly tired, stressed, or off-form? If any of these char-
acteristics apply, can I try to let go of the concerns
that disturb me?

The Word

I read the word of God slowly, a few times over, and I listen to what God is saying to me. (Please turn to the Scripture on the following pages. Inspiration points are there should you need them. When you are ready, return here to continue.)

Conversation

I begin to talk with Jesus about the Scripture I have just read. What part of it strikes a chord in me? Perhaps the words of a friend or a story I have heard recently will slowly rise to the surface of my consciousness. If so, does the story throw light on what the Scripture passage may be trying to say to me?

Conclusion

Glory be to the Father, and to the Son, and to the Holy Spirit,
As it was in the beginning, is now and ever shall be,
World without end. Amen.

Sunday 31st December
The Holy Family of Jesus, Mary and Joseph
Luke 2:22–40

When the time came for their purification accord-ing to the law of Moses, they brought him up to Jerusalem to present him to the Lord (as it is written in the law of the Lord, "Every firstborn male shall be designated as holy to the Lord"), and they offered a sacrifice according to what is stated in the law of the Lord, "a pair of turtle-doves or two young pigeons." Now there was a man in Jerusalem whose name was Simeon; this man was righteous and devout, look-ing forward to the consolation of Israel, and the Holy Spirit rested on him. It had been revealed to him by the Holy Spirit that he would not see death before he had seen the Lord's Messiah. Guided by the Spirit, Simeon came into the temple; and when the parents brought in the child Jesus, to do for him what was customary under the law, Simeon took him in his arms and praised God, saying,

"Master, now you are dismissing your servant in
        peace,
    according to your word;
for my eyes have seen your salvation,
    which you have prepared in the presence of all
        peoples,

a light for revelation to the Gentiles
    and for glory to your people Israel."

And the child's father and mother were amazed at what was being said about him. Then Simeon blessed them and said to his mother Mary, "This child is destined for the falling and the rising of many in Israel, and to be a sign that will be opposed so that the inner thoughts of many will be revealed—and a sword will pierce your own soul too."

There was also a prophet, Anna the daughter of Phanuel, of the tribe of Asher. She was of a great age, having lived with her husband for seven years after her marriage, then as a widow to the age of eighty-four. She never left the temple but worshipped there with fasting and prayer night and day. At that moment she came, and began to praise God and to speak about the child to all who were looking for the redemption of Jerusalem.

When they had finished everything required by the law of the Lord, they returned to Galilee, to their own town of Nazareth. The child grew and became strong, filled with wisdom; and the favor of God was upon him.

- Jesus comes not in splendor, but as a baby in his mother's arms. Lord, I see you here in the vulnerable flesh of a child, a sign that will be spoken against. Already the shadow of Calvary falls on

Mary as Simeon tells her that a sword will pierce her soul.

- Jesus, you share my humanity in every way. Like you, I want to grow and become strong, filled with wisdom. I still have miles to go before I sleep. May the favor of God be with me as with you.

Monday 1st January
The Solemnity of Mary, The Holy Mother of God
Luke 2:16–21

So they went with haste and found Mary and Joseph, and the child lying in the manger. When they saw this, they made known what had been told them about this child; and all who heard it were amazed at what the shepherds told them. But Mary treasured all these words and pondered them in her heart. The shepherds returned, glorifying and praising God for all they had heard and seen, as it had been told them. After eight days had passed, it was time to circumcise the child; and he was called Jesus, the name given by the angel before he was conceived in the womb.

- We start the year, as we start our life, under the protection of a mother. Today we celebrate the most passionate and enduring of all human relationships, that of mother and child. As Mary looked at her baby and gave him her breast, she knew that there was a dimension here beyond her imagining.

• Christians contemplated Mary for three centuries before the Council of Ephesus, when they dared to consecrate the title *qeotokos*, Mother of God. Like Mary, I treasure the words spoken about Jesus, and ponder them in my heart.

Tuesday 2nd January
John 1:19–28

This is the testimony given by John when the Jews sent priests and Levites from Jerusalem to ask him, "Who are you?" He confessed and did not deny it, but confessed, "I am not the Messiah." And they asked him, "What then? Are you Elijah?" He said, "I am not." "Are you the prophet?" He answered, "No." Then they said to him, "Who are you? Let us have an answer for those who sent us. What do you say about yourself?" He said,

"I am the voice of one crying out in the wilderness, 'Make straight the way of the Lord,'"
as the prophet Isaiah said.

Now they had been sent from the Pharisees. They asked him, "Why then are you baptizing if you are neither the Messiah, nor Elijah, nor the prophet?" John answered them, "I baptize with water. Among you stands one whom you do not know, the one who is coming after me; I am not worthy to untie the thong of his sandal." This took place in Bethany across the Jordan where John was baptizing.

- John understood who he was—and who he wasn't. He had a strong sense of the role he played in God's plan. He could not allow his own ego or others' expectations to distract or distort his mission.

- God, I want a better sense of who I am—and who I am not. I want to embrace fully the mission you have for me. I do not want my own ego or others' expectations to get in the way of my walking the path you have set before me.

Wednesday 3rd January
John 1:29–34

The next day he saw Jesus coming towards him and declared, "Here is the Lamb of God who takes away the sin of the world! This is he of whom I said, 'After me comes a man who ranks ahead of me because he was before me.' I myself did not know him; but I came baptizing with water for this reason, that he might be revealed to Israel." And John testified, "I saw the Spirit descending from heaven like a dove, and it remained on him. I myself did not know him, but the one who sent me to baptize with water said to me, 'He on whom you see the Spirit descend and remain is the one who baptizes with the Holy Spirit.' And I myself have seen and have testified that this is the Son of God."

- "Lamb of God" evokes Old Testament passages: of the Passover lamb, and of the Suffering Servant in Isaiah, led like a lamb to the slaughter, bearing our sins.

- Lord, whenever I hear of some atrocious barbarism and of the injustice and pain people suffer through others' wickedness, I remember that this is the world you entered, the burden you took on yourself. You had a strong back to carry the evil that is in the world. Remind me to rely on your strength and compassion.

Thursday 4th January
John 1:35–42

The next day John again was standing with two of his disciples, and as he watched Jesus walk by, he exclaimed, "Look, here is the Lamb of God!" The two disciples heard him say this, and they followed Jesus. When Jesus turned and saw them following, he said to them, "What are you looking for?" They said to him, "Rabbi" (which translated means Teacher), "where are you staying?" He said to them, "Come and see." They came and saw where he was staying, and they remained with him that day. It was about four o'clock in the afternoon. One of the two who heard John speak and followed him was Andrew, Simon Peter's brother. He first found his brother Simon and said to him, "We have found the Messiah" (which is translated Anointed). He brought Simon to Jesus, who looked at him and said, "You are Simon son of John. You are to be called Cephas" (which is translated Peter).

- "What are you looking for?" Such a searching question that is! Many would say, "I'm not looking for anything. I am just trying to survive." But in sober moments we realize that we would like our lives to amount to more than just getting and spending, eating and sleeping.

- Lord, I want you to look at me as you looked at Simon. Invite me to see where you are to be found and to remain with you.

Friday 5th January
John 1:43–51

The next day Jesus decided to go to Galilee. He found Philip and said to him, "Follow me." Now Philip was from Bethsaida, the city of Andrew and Peter. Philip found Nathanael and said to him, "We have found him about whom Moses in the law and also the prophets wrote, Jesus son of Joseph from

Nazareth." Nathanael said to him, "Can anything good come out of Nazareth?" Philip said to him, "Come and see." When Jesus saw Nathanael coming toward him, he said of him, "Here is truly an Israelite in whom there is no deceit!" Nathanael asked him, "Where did you get to know me?" Jesus answered, "I saw you under the fig tree before Philip called you." Nathanael replied, "Rabbi, you are the Son of God! You are the King of Israel!" Jesus answered, "Do you believe because I told you that I saw you under the fig tree? You will see greater things than these." And he said to him, "Very truly, I tell you, you will see heaven opened and the angels of God ascending and descending upon the Son of Man."

- "Can anything good come out of Nazareth?" Nathanael (identified with Bartholomew from the ninth century on) could have missed the chance to meet Jesus, but he heard Philip's gentle invitation, "Come and see."

- How often, Lord, have I tried to pigeon-hole people by looking down at their gender, origin, race, or family. Save me from the stupidity of those who try to seem smart by despising others. May I heed Philip, and "come and see" who you are and what you offer me.

Saturday 6th January
Mark 1:7–11

[John] proclaimed, "The one who is more powerful than I is coming after me; I am not worthy to stoop down and untie the thong of his sandals. I have baptized you with water; but he will baptize you with the Holy Spirit."

In those days Jesus came from Nazareth of Galilee and was baptized by John in the Jordan. And just as he was coming up out of the water, he saw the heavens torn apart and the Spirit descending like a dove on him. And a voice came from heaven, "You are my Son, the Beloved; with you I am well pleased."

- Do we ever consider that Jesus needed to hear these words from his heavenly Father—"You are my Son, the Beloved; with you I am well pleased"? He was about to embark on his ministry. In fact, from this place of baptism he would first be severely tempted in the wilderness. He was divine but also human, and these words from heaven came at the right time.

- Lord, when I realize that you love me and are well pleased with me, I experience true freedom. I can do anything you ask. I can endure whatever is required. I can grow strong in faith and hope and love.

Sunday 7th January
The Epiphany of the Lord
Matthew 2:1–12

In the time of King Herod, after Jesus was born in Bethlehem of Judea, wise men from the East came to Jerusalem, asking, "Where is the child who has been born king of the Jews? For we observed his star at its rising, and have come to pay him homage." When King Herod heard this, he was frightened, and all Jerusalem with him; and calling together all the chief priests and scribes of the people, he inquired of them where the Messiah was to be born. They told him, "In Bethlehem of Judea; for so it has been written by the prophet:

'And you, Bethlehem, in the land of Judah,
    are by no means least among the rulers of
        Judah;'
for from you shall come a ruler
    who is to shepherd my people Israel."

Then Herod secretly called for the wise men and learned from them the exact time when the star had appeared. Then he sent them to Bethlehem, saying, "Go and search diligently for the child; and when you have found him, bring me word so that I may also go and pay him homage." When they had heard the king, they set out; and there, ahead of them, went the star that they had seen at its rising, until it stopped over the place where the child was. When they saw that the star had stopped, they were overwhelmed with joy. On entering the house, they saw the child with Mary his mother; and they knelt down and paid him homage. Then, opening their treasure chests, they offered him gifts of gold, frankincense, and myrrh. And having been warned in a dream not to return to Herod, they left for their own country by another road.

- There is a Bavarian custom of chalking G M B (Gaspar, Melchior, Balthasar) on the wall of each room of the house on Epiphany morning. These are the names that tradition assigns to the Magi, representing all the nations of the world. More and more, the nations of the world move to our shores and come into our homes. If the Magi arrived here today, would they be welcome?

- When people come to my home, Lord, do they discover you there? If justice and love are to be found in my home, then visitors, like the Magi, will be overwhelmed with joy, and they will pay you homage.

Monday 8th January
The Baptism of the Lord
Mark 1:7–11

John proclaimed, "The one who is more powerful than I is coming after me; I am not worthy to stoop down and untie the thong of his sandals. I have baptised you with water; but he will baptize you with the Holy Spirit." In those days Jesus came from Nazareth of Galilee and was baptized by John in the Jordan. And just as he was coming up out of the water, he saw the heavens torn apart and the Spirit descending like a dove on him. And a voice came from heaven, "You are my Son, the Beloved; with you I am well pleased."

- Imagine yourself witnessing the scene, perhaps standing in the shallows, the water flowing around your ankles. Picture the scene and allow it to unfold. What is it like? The young man from Nazareth joins the queue waiting for John's baptism: a symbol of purifying but also of birth—coming up out of the waters of the womb into a new life as God's beloved child.

- Lord, when I realize that you love me and are well pleased with me, it is like the start of a new life. As I hear your voice, I know that I have a purpose and a destiny.

An Advent Retreat

Welcome to this year's Advent retreat. Any retreat offers a chance to take a step back from the pressing concerns of everyday life and to reflect prayerfully on the current state of your relationships—with God, with the people around you, and with the world in which you live. This season of Advent, during which we prepare ourselves to celebrate the coming of Christ at Christmas, is a great opportunity to make a retreat of this kind.

This year, our reflective focus will be on the "O" Antiphons traditionally used in the anticipation of Jesus' coming to dwell among us. You can think of them as seven ways to express Jesus, and they are best known as the sung response that introduces the Magnificat at evening prayer in the final days of Advent. Their origin can be traced back to the prophecies of Isaiah, who tells of the coming Messiah.

We will spend time on each Antiphon, exploring one per session, giving ourselves space to find the richness in each one. So, to get familiar with them, here are the O Antiphons:

O Wisdom
O Sacred Lord
O Shoot of Jesse
O Key of David
O Radiant Dawn

O King of All the Nations
O Emmanuel

After hearing these, you might recognize them from the famous hymn, "O Come O Come Emmanuel," which we hear time and again each Christmas. But have you ever stopped to think about what these names reveal about the nature and character of Jesus? This retreat will help you explore each Antiphon with fresh eyes to see and ears to hear what the Lord has to say to you.

As we begin this Advent journey, we should ask ourselves how the following weeks will bring us closer to Jesus:

• What do you hope to gain from this retreat?

• How do you see Jesus?

• How would you express Jesus if someone asked you to?

• How would you address him?

Practicalities

We start with some practical hints that might help you if you haven't made a retreat like this before, or that might act as reminders if you have. These tips fall under three headings: how, when, and what.

One "how" question to consider is how much time are you able to devote to each session of the retreat?

It's good to decide this in advance and try to stick to your decision. Don't give up too soon if the prayer seems a little dull or continue too long if it seems to be going well. The material presented in each of these presentations lasts 20–25 minutes, but you might want to take a little extra time beforehand to prepare yourself, or some time afterward to stay in prayer. The important thing is to choose a time that you can comfortably fit into your routine.

A good "when" question to ask is what time of day is best for you to pray? Would you seek out time in the morning, evening, or the middle of the day? This might also lead to another question: where will you find it easiest to pray and reflect in this way?

Finally, under the heading of "what," ask yourself what you hope to gain from this retreat. What are the gifts and graces you hope to receive from God during these times of prayer? Make sure you start the prayer by asking God for these or for whatever else God wants to give you.

When you have taken a while to consider these questions, you'll be ready to begin this prayerful time of reflecting on the O Antiphons. Before you begin, just become aware of God welcoming you to meet him in this way. Become aware, also, of all those others around the world who are praying this retreat alongside you.

Session 1 O Wisdom
Stillness Exercise

- Most people can enter more fully into prayer if they take a little time to become more still. At the beginning of each day's prayer, we will suggest a stillness exercise and lead you through it. (Perhaps you will find that one works better than others for you; make note of what was helpful and use it the next time you pray.) Today, let's affirm the wisdom of the body. We often ignore our bodies, but if we listen, the body can speak to us and reveal something that the conscious mind has missed.

- You may be sitting, standing, or walking. Notice how you are in your body. Are you warm or cold? Are you comfortable or not? Relaxed or tense? Pay attention to your feet in contact with the ground and what they are wearing. Work your way from there up to your shoulders, noticing sensations as you go. Do the same with your fingers, hands, arms, up to the shoulders; often we carry tension in the shoulders, so if you notice any, try to let it go. Move to the head and the facial muscles. If there is tension around the eyes, the mouth, or the jaw, you can release it as you breathe out by imagining that you are giving your tension to God: letting go of it into God. Is there anything your body is wanting to say to you today?

Reflect

O Come, Thou Wisdom, from on high,
And order all things, far and nigh;
To us the path of knowledge show,
And cause us in her ways to go.

When we contemplate the Wisdom that comes from on high, we can look back to the very beginning. A play about the Creation story tells the following tale: God was delighted with all that had been made through his word. However, Satan was jealous and schemed to spoil it. Seeing that God's power lay in the word that came from his mouth, Satan said to God, "Let me put a seal on your tongue and tempt this Creation. We shall see how well it fends for itself." Strangely, God agreed. And Satan got to work, tempting human beings to corruption. The effects of sin inspired by Satan were evident to God's eternal eye, and God turned to Satan and held up one finger. Satan understood that God desired to utter just one word and decided to allow it; after all what could one word do in the face of all the evils that had now been wrought and the habit of sin that so imbued humanity? Besides, Satan looked forward to mocking God's impotence. Satan removed the seal on God's tongue, and God prepared to speak a single word and to breathe into that word the totality of his love and the fullness of all Wisdom. And the word that came from the mouth of God . . . was "Jesus."

We hear now of this Wisdom entering our world from the Gospel of Luke.

Reading
Luke 1:26–28, 30b–31

The Angel Gabriel was sent by God to a town in Galilee called Nazareth, to a virgin engaged to a man whose name was Joseph, of the house of David. The virgin's name was Mary. And he came to her and said, "Greetings, favored one! The Lord is with you. . . . Do not be afraid, Mary, for you have found favor with God. And now, you will conceive in your womb and bear a son, and you will name him Jesus."

Talk to God

- The wisdom of God is the child born to a young woman in an unimportant town in a weak nation, with corrupt leaders who collaborated with Rome.

- Consider that response of God. And spend a little time with Mary as she receives this news: "you will conceive in your womb and bear a son, and you will name him Jesus."

- The state of the world can get us down. We long for God to intervene and inspire clear thinking in the minds of all who make important decisions that affect the lives of billions, especially the poor. We want them to be wise.

- Take some time to pray for our secular and religious leaders, to pray that they might be open to the wisdom of God.

- In the celebration of Christmas, we are shown the surprising nature of God's wisdom. God's response to the predicament of the world then and now and always: Jesus.

- What is God showing you through this act of incarnation?

- Christmas is not an escape from a troubled world. It's a time to look again at how God wants to enter the world. The third verse of the Christmas carol, "O Little town of Bethlehem" goes:

How silently, how silently,
    The wondrous gift is given!
So God imparts to human hearts
    The blessings of His Heaven.
No ear may hear His coming;
    But in this world of sin,
Where meek souls will receive Him still,
    The dear Christ enters in.

- How do you want to respond to this God who enters in?

Session 2 O Sacred Lord
Stillness Exercise

- Today, we will repeat a very important word to help you into stillness. Notice where you are, how you are, what is going on for you, and give all that to God.

- Ask for what you seek in this prayer. For example, it might be to know Jesus as Lord.

- Then take the Aramaic word *Maranatha,* which means "Come, O Lord" and repeat that word as you breathe: *Maranatha.* Do this for a couple of minutes. If you become distracted, simply return to the word.

Reflect

- The disciples sometimes called Jesus, Lord. This might be one of your names for him. It is a name Jesus seems willing to apply to himself on occasion.

- The word denotes authority and calls to mind Jesus' words at the end of Matthew's Gospel: "All authority in heaven and on earth has been given to me." His final sentence is just as consoling: "And remember, I am with you always, to the end of the age."

- So, he will be with us, and all authority is his. In these dark days of winter, we have no need to fear.

- Let the Lord Jesus be with you. What does he want you to know? What do you want him to know?

Reading

- At the end of the 14th Century, when Europe was in the grip of the plague and many feared the world was coming to an end, Julian of Norwich, mystic and theologian, shared her image of God with a troubled world. She affirmed that whatever disasters befall us, whatever challenges we face, Jesus is Lord and is always with us.

- Julian has an assured sense of God saying, "All shall be well, and all shall be well, and all manner of thing shall be well."

- Julian shares more of what she hears God say to her and to all of us:

"See I am God: See that I am in all things: See that I do all things: See that I have never left the hands of my works, nor never shall without end: See that I lead all things to the end that I ordain it to, for without beginning, by the same might, wisdom, and love that I made it with, How should anything be amiss?"

Talk to God

- This is an invitation to trust in the providence of God. We do not need to be frantic in our efforts to put right what is wrong in the world.

- Return to your saying of the word *Maranatha*. As you breathe out, let go of some of the anxiety about life you may be carrying around.

- Remember that trust in providence is not a license to be passive. I may not conclude that because Jesus is Lord, I need do nothing. Not at all! We are called to a middle way in which we hear Jesus, our Lord, call us to work with him for the good of the world.

- How is Jesus calling you to work with him for the good of the world? Listen to him. Respond to him.

- Because we can be utterly confident in him, we can trust less in distracting worldly securities. We can become more generous with our time, talents, and wealth. Does this notion inspire a petition in you, perhaps to be more trusting and less distracted? *Maranatha* . . . Come O Lord.

Session 3 O Shoot of Jesse; O Flower of Jesse's Stem

Stillness Exercise

- If you are near a window, look outside. If not, consider nature at this time of year. What kind of a day is it? What do you see or imagine? If it is wintry, just be present to it for a while.

- If you wish, go outside and find a leafless tree, or withered flower, or any other thing that speaks to you of winter's unresponsiveness. And let it be whatever it is.

Reading

- In Isaiah we read, "But a shoot shall come out from the stump of Jesse, and a branch shall grow out of his roots." Jesse was the father of king David, and the Jews believed that the Messiah would come from David's line. Christians understand Jesus as the fulfillment of that prophecy. The stump of Jesse represents the ancestors of Jesus. And Jesus himself is a shoot that will become a flowering branch, bursting into life.

- In Luke's Gospel, Zechariah, the father of John the Baptist, speaks of what God is doing at that time through Jesus (and also John).

Luke 1:67–79

Then his father Zechariah was filled with the Holy Spirit and spoke this prophecy:

"Blessed be the Lord God of Israel,
>   for he has looked favorably on his people and redeemed them.

He has raised up a mighty savior for us
>   in the house of his servant David,

as he spoke through the mouth of his holy prophets from of old,
>   that we would be saved from our enemies and from the hand of all who hate us.

Thus he has shown the mercy promised to our ancestors,
>   and has remembered his holy covenant,

the oath that he swore to our ancestor Abraham,
>   to grant us that we, being rescued from the hands of our enemies,

might serve him without fear, in holiness and righteousness
>   before him all our days.

And you, child, will be called the prophet of the Most High;
>   for you will go before the Lord to prepare his ways,

to give knowledge of salvation to his people
>   by the forgiveness of their sins.

By the tender mercy of our God,
    the dawn from on high will break upon us,
to give light to those who sit in darkness and in the
        shadow of death,
    to guide our feet into the way of peace."

Reflect

- In the Northern hemisphere, we are in the depths of winter. Little grows. Trees and shrubs lie dormant. Most flowers are long gone. The external scene can affect our own soul. We can feel pretty lifeless in the middle of winter. And the winter can symbolize the state of our own souls or even the state of humanity in the grip of dereliction.

- Where in the world or the church or your own self is there a corresponding lack of life and color?

- Under the ground, nature bides her time but is not idle. Bulbs send out roots, seeds vernalize in the frosts and break open, ready for warmer weather. (We may recall Jesus saying: "Unless a grain of wheat falls to the ground and dies, it remains just a single grain; but if it dies, it bears much fruit."). The roots of trees are active still, searching for and retaining goodness in the soil, preparing to fuel spring growth.

- This is a good image for prayer, especially when nothing or very little seems to be happening. If it is dry, can you let it be what it is, and trust that

God knows what he's doing? Rest in that God for a while. Don't force the shoots of spring. Let yourself be who you are, and where you are. And let Jesus be who he is.

Talk to God

Now the winter is past,
>   the rain is over and gone.
The flowers appear on the earth;
>   the time of singing has come,
and the voice of the turtle-dove
>   is heard in our land.
The fig tree puts forth its figs,
>   and the vines are in blossom;
>   they give forth fragrance.

—Song of Solomon 2:11–13

Session 4 O Key of David
Stillness Exercise

- Do you have keys on your person or near at hand? Go get them. Hold the key or multiple keys in your hand. Look at them. Feel the weight of them. Notice their shape, size, color, temperature, and anything else about them.

- What are they for? What associations do they have for you? How do they describe your life, responsibilities, gifts, burdens?

- Hold them. Look at them. Let God look at them. And let God look at you.

Reading

- The world is full of need. We can easily become paralyzed in the face of so many needs and demands, oppressed by the weight of it all, and unable to see a path through dark woods. Jesus reminds us that he is that path. As he says in John's Gospel (14:1–7):

> "Do not let your hearts be troubled. Believe in God, believe also in me. In my Father's house there are many dwelling-places. If it were not so, would I have told you that I go to prepare a place for you? And if I go and prepare a place for you, I will come again and will take you to myself, so that where I am, there you may be also. And you know the way to the place where I am going." Thomas said to him, "Lord, we do not know where you are going. How can we know the way?" Jesus said to him, "I am the way, and the truth, and the life. No one comes to the Father except through me. If you know me, you will know my Father also. From now on you do know him and have seen him."

Reflect

- Jesus is the way, or the path, and the key that opens the gates of the kingdom. Jesus gave the keys of the kingdom of heaven to Peter. In some sense, we all share in that vocation given to Peter. God gives to each of us a way of opening a door for other people. The way is always the same Jesus. And yet, each one of us has a particular way of giving witness to Jesus because of our unique experience of him. We each have a unique key.

- What is it that you have seen in Jesus that you want to share with the world?

- Your particular personality, your gifts, your circumstances—YOU—can reveal something new about Jesus. You can show something about him that has not yet been seen. This could be a key that unlocks a door for others.

- When Jesus calls a person, it is always to be a disciple; this is the universal call. It is also an invitation to be the disciple you are particularly called to be. This is your particular key. This idea was championed by Herbert Alfonso in his fine book: *The Personal Vocation*. He argued that a clue—or might we say—a key to your personal vocation is whatever gives you life, and energy, and brings light to your own soul. It will be confirmed if it is also fruitful for others in various ways.

Talk to God

- So, what is it that brings you life and light and energy? Talk to Jesus about this. Is there a key here to your own personal vocation?

- Vocation is always about being with Jesus and being sent out by him.

- Discernment invites me to consider where I am being called to find my own creative way of loving. Since I cannot do everything, what is it in particular that I might do in this world of need? Which door does God want me to unlock? This is personal vocation. It is in relationship with Jesus, the key, that we are most able to discover how this personal vocation wants to express itself in our lives. Jesus unlocks something in us so that the door is opened to our particular way of loving. This is why Jesus is himself the key to the kingdom of heaven that always wants to come to earth, incarnating in each of us, and in me, as I hear his call and respond to him.

- Do you know what your personal vocation is? Ask Jesus to show you.

Session 5 O Radiant Dawn, O Dayspring

Stillness Exercise

- When you are cold, you might stand before the sun and let its warmth bathe you. A suggestion of St Ignatius is a spiritual version of that. He suggests that before we begin a time of prayer we stand for about a minute and let God gaze at us. This is the God who made you and loves you.

- So, take a minute now. Stand up if you can, or remain sitting if that makes more sense. Be still, and let God look at you, or be with you, in any way that God wants.

Reflect

- At the winter solstice we experience the shortest days and longest nights of the year. However dark the night, Jesus shines as a radiant dawn.

- Sometimes we experience this affectively (that is, we feel it) and we are consoled. Other times we hold onto it in faith even though our own dark night obscures the feeling of consolation.

- This is still a consolation although less affective (or less of a felt experience). We might call it a "head consolation" rather than a "heart consolation."

- In your life of faith at the moment, are you experiencing some consolation? Is it of the heart (affective) or of the head (non-affective)?

Reading

- Sometimes God allows a certain dryness or darkness in our lives—but we are not abandoned. God is still there, and God's light is still there. It is just that we cannot perceive that light.

- St. John of the Cross wrote, in *Dark Night of the Soul*: "In this dark night of the desire (to the end that the words of the Prophet may be fulfilled, namely: 'Thy light shall shine in the darkness'), God will enlighten the soul, giving it knowledge, not only of its lowliness and wretchedness, as we have said, but likewise of the greatness and excellence of God."

- And in Psalm 139:11–12, we read: "If I say, 'Surely the darkness shall cover me, / and the light around me become night', / even the darkness is not dark to you; / the night is as bright as the day, / for darkness is as light to you."

Talk to God

- Where are you sensing the light of Christ in your life? Delight in that sense. Breathe it in.

- Are there darker places you don't want God to see? Do you dare to show Jesus those parts of yourself?

- How does Jesus want to bring his healing light, to bathe you in the warmth of his love? Can you let him do that?

Session 6 O King of All the Nations
Stillness Exercise

- Take a look back over your day or, if it makes more sense, the last twenty-four hours: Where have you been? What have you done? With whom? How did it go?

- Notice where there was the most life, light, and energy. Notice where life, light, or energy drained from you.

- Where was God at work in you or around you in the last day? What gifts did the day bring? Was there a nugget of gold hidden in your day? Talk to God about what you notice.

Reading
Matthew's nativity describes the wise men bringing gold to Jesus, for this child is a king. Yet, the actual absence of luxury tells us something important about our God. The life Jesus will live will tell us even more. He chooses a way of humility.

St. Paul reminds us of that humility of Jesus in his letter to the Philippians (2:1–11):

If then there is any encouragement in Christ, any consolation from love, any sharing in the Spirit, any compassion and sympathy, make my joy complete: be of the same mind, having the same love, being in full accord and of one mind. Do nothing from selfish ambition or conceit, but in humility regard others as better than yourselves. Let each of you look not to your own interests, but to the interests of others. Let the same mind be in you that was in Christ Jesus,

who, though he was in the form of God,
　　did not regard equality with God
　　as something to be exploited,
but emptied himself,
　　taking the form of a slave,
　　being born in human likeness.
And being found in human form,
　　he humbled himself
　　and became obedient to the point of death—
　　even death on a cross.
Therefore God also highly exalted him
　　and gave him the name
　　that is above every name,
so that at the name of Jesus
　　every knee should bend,
　　in heaven and on earth and under the earth,

and every tongue should confess
    that Jesus Christ is Lord,
    to the glory of God the Father.

Reflect
The Kingdom
Part One

- Imagine our present world with all its problems and needs and hopes. Perhaps one area of need strikes you most.

- Now imagine that someone emerges with a hope, a plan, and a way of putting things right. They have all the qualities needed to make this work. They have the vision and the realism to see it through. Use your imagination to see this person: What they look like? Picture their clothes, their demeanor, their home. Listen to them as they go about their life. What is their plan? What is their project? How are they going to go about putting their plan into action? How do they speak to others? What are their qualities? What is their style. . . ?

- Imagine that this special person has everything they need to inspire you to follow them. Can you say what those gifts are? Can you imagine following and working with them, even though doing so will lead to hardship?

- Now imagine this person addressing a large gathering and presenting their project, with you in the audience. Listen to them; watch them. What appeal do they make? What words do they use?

- Then imagine everyone else has left but you. You sit alone. You wonder what kind of person could reject such an appeal. What kind of person would accept? What about you? Suppose you left too. What would that make you?

- After a while, move to part two.

Talk to God
The Kingdom
Part Two

- If someone such as the person I have been imagining could attract me so, how much more could Jesus attract me?

- Imagine Jesus seated with his seventy-two disciples. They sit on a hill. Look at them. What do they see in Jesus that inspires them to follow him? Then look at Jesus himself. Take in how he dresses, how he holds himself, the look in his eyes, and the tone of his voice. Could you be inspired by this man? What qualities would Jesus need to have for you to be inspired? What would his project have to be to catch your imagination? What does he dream that has the power to ignite your soul?

- Listen to him now. What would he say that could inspire you to want to give him your loyalty?

- Then consider that, while anyone with any sense would want to follow this man Jesus, some might want to follow him so closely in his enterprise as to be with him wherever he goes and whatever he does; to stand with him no matter what; to go with him and share his burdens and joys, his triumphs and failures.

- What do you want to say to that Jesus now?

Session 7 O Emmanuel

Stillness Exercise

- Let's use your breathing to enter stillness today. Begin by noticing your breath, the sound of it, and the rhythm. There is no need to change the rate.

- Notice the air as it enters your body, fills your lungs, sustains your life, and then departs.

- As you inhale, breathe in God's love for you. As you exhale, breathe out anything you want to share with God, or let go of and hand over to God. Take three deeper breaths doing this.

Reflection

- The reality of suffering is a problem for any religion. We would like God to put an end to suffering, but at what cost? Would it not mean the end of creation as we know it? The termination of the human project? It would have been easier surely to have never begun the enterprise. Creation was always going to invite suffering. The creation of intelligent beings would also mean the reality of evil. If God was determined to breathe life into the beings he had made, he was asking for trouble. There could be no other way. However, if God entered creation and became human too, that might make a difference. Then, at least we would not be alone. Perhaps that would even be enough, or at least helpful. Suffering and evil would still exist, but God would be with us. "God with us." *Emmanuel.*

- Are you able to face an arena of suffering humanity today? It might be your own pain or the suffering of others. Where is God in this? Where does God want to be?

Reading

- [W]hy should God have made [people] at all, if He had not intended them to know Him? But, in fact, the good God has given them a share in His own Image, that is, in our Lord Jesus Christ, and has made even themselves after the same Image and Likeness. Why? Simply in order that through this gift of Godlikeness in themselves they may be able to perceive the Image Absolute, that is the Word Himself, and through Him to apprehend the Father; which knowledge of their Maker is for men the only really happy and blessed life.

—St. Athanasius, On the Incarnation

Talk to God

- Can you imagine this scene? Humanity is in desolation, and the Trinity looks on. Jesus asks to be sent to earth in spite of what that would mean. Watch him turn to the Father and make his request: "Let me go there."

- *Emmanuel.* God with us. What do you want to say to this Jesus?

Conclusion
Look back over the retreat

- Looking back over the journey you have taken during the past few weeks is always an important part of making a retreat such as this one. It is highly possible that you now see Jesus with fresh eyes or have encountered him in a new way.

- You might recall the prompting questions from the introduction at the beginning of this retreat:

  - What do you hope to gain from this retreat?

  - How do you see Jesus?

  - How would you express Jesus if someone asked you to?

  - How would you address him?'

- Has your picture of Jesus changed in some way during this retreat?

- Perhaps there was a particular session that stood out for you. Which was it? Why?

- By way of summary, we will name the O Antiphons again, with a pause and a few words of prompting in between to help you recall the important moments you had with God in each session.

O Wisdom . . . "Jesus," the one word that came from the mouth of God

O Sacred Lord . . . the authority of God

O Shoot of Jesse . . . a shoot that will become a flower bursting into life

O Key of David . . . the path and way to the kingdom of heaven

O Radiant Dawn . . . the light that comes into the darkness

O King of all the Nations . . . the servant king

O Emmanuel . . . God with us

- In these last few moments, reflect on how God has spoken to you in this retreat. Bring to him all that has been good, and all that has been a struggle for you. You might like to talk to Jesus, addressing him through whichever Antiphon has meant the most to you.

- Bring all this to the Messiah; God with us. *Maranatha* . . . Come, Lord Jesus.